Pacific Nor

TRAIL COOK BOOK

Trail Cooks' Favorite Recipes

John and Roberta Wolcott

Features Northwest
5132 - 126th Place N.E.
Marysville, Washington 98270

Original Pen and Ink Artwork
By
R. "Alec" Malmstead

Other Artwork Courtesy of
Washington Outfitters & Guides Association
Redmond, Washington

Printed by
Snohomish Publishing Company
Snohomish, Washington

First Edition January 1991
Second Printing - August 1991

ISBN 0-931435-04-8

Table of Contents

Introduction..............................Page 1

Trail Cooks Create Memorable
Wilderness Meals...................Page 3

Cooking With Coals........................Page 7

Dutch Ovens - Cooking and
Seasoning..........................Page 9

About The Trail Cooks.....................Page 11

TRAIL RECIPES

Breakfasts

Sausage and Egg Casserole..........Page 16
Dutch Oven Breakfast...............Page 17
Biscuits and Gravy.................Page 18
Sourdough Waffles..................Page 19
Ann's Sourdough Starter............Page 20
Ann's Sourdough Pancakes...........Page 20
Andy's Sourdough Pancakes..........Page 21
Pasayten Stew......................Page 22

Lunch

"Sit-On" Turkey Sandwich...........Page 23

Appetizers

Hot Chili Dip......................Page 24
Shrimp Cheese Dip..................Page 24
Chorizo Cheese Ball................Page 25

Salads

Fruit Salad........................Page 26
Cabbage Salad......................Page 27
Apple-Raisin Salad.................Page 28
Old-Fashioned Cabbage Salad........Page 29
Peas & Peanut Slaw.................Page 30

Breads

Sourdough Biscuits.................Page 31
Trail French Bread.................Page 32
Mountain Toast.....................Page 33
Sheepherder's Bread................Page 34
Dutch Oven Coffee Cake.............Page 35
Baking Powder Biscuits.............Page 36

Main Dishes & Dinners

Basque Chicken.....................Page 37
Dutch Oven Chicken
Enchiladas....................Page 38
Macaroni Casserole.................Page 39
Methow Chicken
& Bedsprings..................Page 40
Stuffed Chiles.....................Page 41
Tortilla-Beef Casserole............Page 42
First Night Chili Stew.............Page 44
Campfire Beans.....................Page 45
Oriental Curry.....................Page 46
Hamburger Casserole................Page 47
Fourth of July Stew................Page 48
Roast Beef/Baron of Beef...........Page 49
Onion Casserole....................Page 50
Dorothy's Chili....................Page 51
Burgundy Beef......................Page 52
Chicken Linguine...................Page 53
Teriyaki Chicken and Rice..........Page 54
Colorado Beans.....................Page 55
Chicken & Dumplings................Page 56

Desserts

Dump Cake..........................Page 58
Wranglers' Dump Cake...............Page 59
Elsie's Fruit Cobbler..............Page 60
Wilderness Doughnuts...............Page 62
Chocolate Trail Cake...............Page 63
Sourdough Chocolate Cake...........Page 64
Crouton Cobbler....................Page 65
Chocolate Raspberry Cake...........Page 66
Apple Crisp........................Page 66
No-Bake Oatmeal Cookies............Page 67
Applesauce Upside-Down
Gingerbread........................Page 68

About The Washington Outfitters
& Guides Association...............Page 69

Washington Outfitters
& Guides Association Members.......Page 70

Pacific Northwest Guide and Outfitter
Associations.......................Page 72

About The Authors..................Page 73

To Order Additional Copies of
TRAIL COOK BOOK....................Page 74

Trail Notes

Introduction

The first thought of publishing this book came while we were gathering trail cook interviews, favorite trail recipes and cooking tips for a story on trail cooks published in the May/June 1990 issue of Northwest Living! magazine.

As we were discussing the article with Robert Hult and Frances Brewster, owners of the Last Trading Post in Winthrop, Washington, Robert suggested expanding the magazine idea into a cookbook for riders, hunters, campers or chefs who just like cooking on their home range. We liked the idea -- and here's the result!

Whether you already enjoy Dutch oven cooking, simply want to learn or just want to adapt some of these recipes for your kitchen oven, chances are you'll enjoy this collection of recipes.

Each year hundreds of people discover or re-discover the adventure of horseback rides, llama treks, camping or hunting trips into the high country of the Northwest's mountain regions. For those who take guided trips, some of the favorite memories they bring home with them are thoughts of the great meals served up by their trail cooks.

To share some of these trail meal "secrets", more than 50 recipes from a dozen trail cooks have been gathered for your enjoyment. Many of these recipes are original and had not been written down before.

The assistance of the Washington Outfitters and Guides Association (W.O.G.A.) and many of the trail chefs who ride and cook for Association outfitters has made this book not only possible but fun.

For those of you who have never tried Dutch oven cooking, this book is a fine introduction to one of the most versatile forms of home, backyard or trail cooking. Like any trail trip, wilderness cooking is an adventure. It's a creative style of cooking, not an exacting art.

Don't be afraid to experiment. Many of these recipes include adaptations or variations given by the cooks. Enjoy the results and gather your own collection of favorite Dutch oven recipes.

Remember that the number of servings given for each recipe is based on hearty appetites that have been sharpened by fresh air and physical activity.

You will enjoy not only the recipes, but also the enthusiasm of the trail cooks and the stories they have to tell.

We hope that you will make this book your cooking companion for your own camping, hunting or picnic outings!

THE COOK TENT

Trail Cooks Create Memorable Wilderness Meals

WANTED: Culinary magician to prepare roasts, ribs, chicken, chili, dumplings, cakes and breads to feed a dozen people for three to six days. Pleasant scenic working environment, except when it rains or snows. No electricity or running water. Nearest store, 24 miles by horse trail. If interested, send references to Washington Outfitters and Guides Association, 22845 NE 8th, Suite 331, Redmond, WA 98053.

That's the kind of classified ad that appeals only to trail cooks, the well-seasoned mountain chefs who know how to keep outfitters' camping guests happily fed even in remote wilderness areas.

These food artisans prepare a Dutch oven breakfast of bacon, eggs and hash browns; a Basque chicken dinner, or applesauce upside-down gingerbread dessert in places where cooking on the "range" means a campfire in a mountain wilderness and "turning the heat up" means tossing a couple more grey briquets on top of the Dutch oven.

Washington's trail cooks pride themselves on their reputation for providing memorable meals even in the midst of tall timber and rocky mountain peaks. Their favorite recipes and cooking secrets can add flavor to your own outings.

Sometimes they can even spin off one recipe from another. Take the "Sit-On" Turkey Sandwich for instance, a specialty of trail cook and outfitter Debby Gallie-Miller, whose High Country Outfitters guides guests into the Teanaway Valley and Alpine Lakes regions of the

Cascade Mountains east of Seattle.

"You cut a large round loaf of sourdough French bread in half, then hollow it out and fill it with a high mound of sliced turkey, pastrami, tomatoes, olives and such. Then, replace the top and sit on it!," she laughs. Cut into wedges, it serves six people. The bread that was scooped out can be used the next morning for her Dutch oven sausage and egg casserole.

Sarah Parrington of Kingston, Wa., cooks regularly for Steve Darwood's Cascade Wilderness Outfitters based in Carlton, in north central Washington.

She prefers outdoor cooking to tent-sheltered stoves, enjoying the art of using wood coals under and on top of her cast iron Dutch ovens.

"My chili stew with ground beef and Polish sausage is a favorite," Sarah says. "It's a rich, thick hearty recipe for the first night on the trail and only takes one pot," says Sarah. She rounds out the meal with a green salad spruced up with artichoke hearts, plus hard French rolls and strawberry shortcake for dessert.

Marva Mountjoy of Winthrop, Wa., has cooked for Claude Miller's North Cascade Safari in Winthrop for eight years. She loves to see people's smiling reactions to her Basque Chicken, a recipe derived from her Basque heritage.

"Besides having delicious recipes, it's important to think about how you pack your food, whether it's for a trail trip or a family picnic," she says.

"I use kitchen boxes my husband Jim built to haul my pans, kitchen utensils and food supplies. Boxes lined with styrofoam keep food frozen. The first night's supper is on top and meat frozen at a commercial freezer is on the bottom, since it won't be used for several days. Vegetables can be kept cool by packing them near to the frozen meats but some, like broccoli, don't keep long," she says.

Marva cooks on a traditional sheepherder's stove in the base camp cook tent.

Her stove is fabricated from a discarded airplane gas tank. A broad, flat side of the tank provides a large stovetop heated by a wood fire built inside the tank.

The fire also warms a smaller side water tank attached to the stove to provide a warming surface for food trays and coffee pots while the rest of the meal is cooking. A spigot on the tank provides heated water for hot chocolate or for dish washing.

Andy Mills, who cooks for Steve Darwood's Cascade Wilderness Outfitters, adds a bit of showmanship for camp guests by stacking his Dutch ovens five or six high, heating them with charcoal briquets between each one.

At the Washington Outfitters & Guides Association Packers Rendezvous at Winthrop in May 1990, Mills stacked six ovens concealing an Australian pot pie of beef and tomatoes in the bottom oven, topped by ovens filled with green beans, sourdough biscuits (two ovens), a cherry cake and a cherry topping for the cake.

"It takes a lot of coordinating," Mills says, "but briquets are a very uniform heat source and you can get very accurate with them."

For Charles Morrison of Kent, Wa., who cooks for outfitter Brian Varrelman of Peteros, Wa., a camp stove with a baking oven provides a versatile base camp kitchen. He produces such favorite wilderness fare as chicken and dumplings, complete with potatoes, carrots, peas, corn, green peppers and garlic.

Marianne LeSage of North Cascade Outfitters in Brewster, Wa., believes Dutch ovens are worth packing into the Pasayten Wilderness despite their weight.

"You always have a campfire so you always have coals for the Dutch ovens. People are fascinated when you lift the lid off an oven and there's a Mexican pizza casserole, peach cobbler or a Dutch oven breakfast," says Marianne.

Dutch ovens have a long Western tradition, she says. Wagon trains carried them from the East and cowboys used them on trail drives. Today, that Old West tradition is still part of the New West lifestyle for cowboy outfitters and trail cooks.

Signing on for a trail trip with any of the outfitters listed in the back of this book will provide a memorable trip in the Northwest's abundantly scenic and breathtaking outdoors.

But you'll also collect memories of some of the finest trail food anywhere in the West. The quality of the meals, usually as memorable as the scenery on a high country pack trip, is a pleasant surprise to those who expected beef jerky, hot dogs and lukewarm beans!

-DUTCH OVENS AT WORK-

Parts of this section include excerpts from "The Delicious Secrets of Super Campfire Cooking," an article about trail cooks written by John and Roberta Wolcott for Northwest Living! magazine's May/June 1990 issue.

Cooking With Coals

Using charcoal briquets for camp cooking provides a proven method of heating that can be controlled by the number of briquets and the distance between them. Briquets provide uniform, accurate heat.

To start, build a fire with wood. If it's a grassy area, cut out a piece of sod, roll it up, water it and set it aside so it can be replaced when you're finished.

Then, place the charcoal on the fire. After they've started, remove them with a shovel.

If you have the luxury of a wood-burning camp stove, place the briquets in the wood fire and remove them with tongs when they've started burning.

According to Debby Gallie-Miller, to create a 350 degree oven with briquets, a temperature you'll use for many of these recipes, place grey, heated coals spaced one and a half to two inches apart under the bottom of the oven. That's a good rule-of-thumb that works for figuring the right amount of coals for any size oven. Then use the same spacing rule when you place coals on the lid.

A certain amount of experimenting will be necessary until you become accustomed to cooking with briquets. This rule-of-thumb should help you get started successfully, though. Trail cook Andy Mills offers a tip for cooking with coals. He discovered that when you lift the bail of the oven, if you can hold your hand under the bail and over the lid coals for seven to eight seconds, your oven is heated to about 350 degrees.

Remember that weather conditions play a large role in determining how many briquets to use. If it's a warm sunny day and the ground is dry, use fewer coals. If the weather is cool and the ground is damp, use more briquets, with one and a half inch spacing rather than two inches.

Also, if the weather is cool, spread a piece of aluminum foil on damp ground before placing your coals for the oven bottom. Otherwise, the ground will leech all of the heat from the coals.

Pre-heating the oven in damp weather is even more important for successful cooking than in dry weather. But some trail cooks recommend pre-heating the Dutch oven regardless of the weather. Pre-heating the Dutch oven offers the same advantages as pre-heating your home oven before baking.

When you're cooking with more than one Dutch oven, you may want to try stacking the ovens on top of each other. A single stack of pots can produce a whole meal -- from the main course to dessert -- at the same time, using fewer briquets than for individual ovens.

But you'll have to do some careful pre-planning. The food in the bottom oven has to take the longest cooking time and the top one the least time or you'll be tearing the stack apart trying to see how everything is doing. By sagely juggling the cooking times of each dish on the menu everything will be ready for the meal at the proper time. It takes real skill! (And, lots of experience!)

Naturally, you place the largest oven on the bottom and build the stack with the smallest oven always on top. The first oven is prepared with briquets placed underneath, as mentioned previously. The coals spaced around the lid of the bottom pot -- one and a half to two inches apart -- will also be about the right number for heating the next pot that's resting on top of the lid.

If you don't have briquets for your Dutch ovens, or run out of them, use hot coals from your wood fire. Hard woods make the best coals, particularly oak -- if you can find it -- and alder. Some woods -- such as white fir and soft pine -- make hot coals but don't hold the heat long. They fall apart or go out while you're cooking, so they must constantly be replaced.

Also, your cooking time -- with wood coals or briquets -- will differ according to the elevation at camp. Because there is less oxygen at higher elevations, coals will vary in the amount of heat they produce.

Dutch Ovens – Cooking and Seasoning

Although some cookbooks tell you not to lift a Dutch oven lid while cooking (to keep the heat in) many trail chefs prefer to peek at their creation, according to Debby Gallie-Miller. Even though she likes to lift the lid for a look, she claims the best test for telling when the dish is done is your nose. "When the food begins to smell divine and makes you start licking your lips, it's about done," she says.

Various Dutch oven sizes serve a predictable number of people and are good for specific types of dishes. For instance, a 10-inch oven is fine for two people and cooks vegetable dishes well.

A 12-inch Dutch oven usually serves up to four people and is fine for baking cakes, breads and desserts.

A 14-inch Dutch oven provides enough food for a large family or a hungry trail crew. Using a 16-inch oven, for large crowds, requires more heat and cooks a little differently than the 10-inch to 14-inch ovens so be prepared to experiment to get used to it.

Whenever you're baking in a Dutch oven, line it with heavy-duty aluminum foil so you can remove your cake or bread easily.

You can buy either cast iron or cast aluminum

Dutch ovens but if weight isn't a problem for you, cast iron will give better performance. Cast iron pots hold heat longer and distribute it more evenly. Trail cook Debby Gallie-Miller says she has baked in each type of oven, side by side using the same recipe. The cake in the cast iron oven came out "perfect" but the one from the cast aluminum oven came out "lop-sided".

If you're doing a lot of cooking with Dutch ovens, particularly stacking them, you may want to use a long hook to lift oven lids, or for moving the Dutch ovens themselves when they're hot. It can be difficult finding the right types of heavy-duty hooks in hardware or retail stores. So most trail cooks just find a blacksmith to make one for them. Steel tongs are great for handling the charcoal.

After you have cooked in your Dutch oven, proper cleaning and care is next.

To clean and season your Dutch oven, fill it with enough water to cover stuck-on food and place it over the campfire until the sticking food comes loose. After you wipe it clean and dry with a paper towel, cure it with a rubbed-on coating of shortening.

Properly cared for Dutch ovens will give generations of good cooking and enjoyment.

About The Trail Cooks

For BILL BUCHANAN of Chelan, Washington, becoming a professional trail cook just sort of came naturally. A hunter and rider all of his life, Bill was usually the one to wind up doing the cooking. So with his well-developed trail-cooking talents, Bill was a natural to become trail cook for his life-long friend Bruce Wick when Bruce and wife Sandy started their Icicle Outfitters & Guides, Inc., seven years ago.

The fantastically beautiful scenery of the high mountain back country and the wonderful sense of freedom are among the things that keep ANN FONKEN of Renton, Washington, coming back each year as a trail cook for Debby Gallie-Miller and Swede Miller's High Country Outfitters. The four years Ann has been camp cooking have been filled with a wonderful blend of memorable people and places.

For DEBBY GALLIE-MILLER, trail cooking began in a surprising way when she took her three children and horses into the Cascade mountains for a summer vacation. A friend who owned an outfitting business had his base camp nearby and asked if she'd like to lend a hand cooking the meals. After agreeing to cook, she discovered the guests for the overnight trip were eight dads and their sons! Then the outfitter handed her a Dutch oven. She'd never even seen one before! Now, nine years and hundreds of Dutch oven meals later, she and husband Swede operate their own outfitting business, High Country Outfitters of Redmond, Washington -- the same business Debby cooked for and then bought from the outfitter who first handed her that Dutch oven!

ANN HENRY of Twisp, Washington, has been a cook for Claude Miller's North Cascade Safari since 1972. One of the things Ann enjoys about the trips is the nice people she meets. And what's even better is that many come back year after year -- it's like seeing old friends each time. Ann finds being a trail cook the perfect way for her to be able to spend time in the mountains she loves.

MARIANNE LeSAGE of Brewster, Washington, got started as a trail cook on family backpacking trips. Then when Marianne and husband Russell purchased a horse packing business in 1980, she became a professional camp cook. Friend Debby Gallie-Miller got her started on Dutch oven cooking about seven years ago. Marianne has adapted many of her old recipes to Dutch Ovens and created new ones.

Ten years ago, ANN MILLER of Twisp, Washington, and her husband Fred rode with friend Claude Miller into the Pasayten Wilderness to help him set up his base camp at the start of the season. Then the cook arrived and invited Ann to "give a hand and help cook". That was all it took to start her career as a trail cook. Ann hasn't missed a season in those 10 years cooking for Claude Miller's North Cascade Safari.

ANDY MILLS of Ellensburg, Washington, first cooked in an elk hunting camp near there around 1983. Steve Darwood, owner of Cascade Wilderness Outfitters, sampled Andy's cooking one fall and then invited him to cook for Darwood's guests on his horsepacking trips.

Andy began cooking for Steve's guests during the 1989 season and says he'd like to cook wilderness meals all of the time if he could earn a full-time living at it.

CHARLES MORRISON of Kent, Washington, began learning about trail cooking by watching his dad during family camping and hunting trips. Later, Chuck got more experience working as a cook for his uncle's logging operation. Then, after being a hunting client of outfitter Brian Varrelman for several years, Brian asked Chuck to cook for him and represent him at the W.O.G.A. Packers Rendezvous '89 in Winthrop. Chuck not only loves trail cooking but does it so that he can spend more time riding and enjoying being in the mountains.

MARVA MOUNTJOY of Winthrop, Washington, began cooking for Claude Miller's North Cascade Safari when Claude was looking for someone to prepare meals for a guest with a special wheat-free diet. Marva has continued cooking for eight years for Claude so that she can ride in the mountains and keep sharing that beautiful mountain world with the guests that join them.

Not a professional cook, but a very experienced trail cook describes DOROTHY NOBLITT of Marysville, Washington. Born in Texas and still a Texan at heart, Dorothy has been the camp cook for many years as her family camped and enjoyed the scenery of several midwest and western states. Dorothy and husband Gene are chili aficionados and have a collection of chili recipes.

For SARAH PARRINGTON of Kingston, Washington, being a trail cook gives her the chance to combine some of her favorite things -- horseback riding, cooking and spending time in the mountains. Eight years ago Sarah started cooking for North Cascade Outfitters, and since then has cooked for Steve Darwood's Cascade Wilderness Outfitters, Aaron Burkhart's Early Winters Outfitting, Brian Varrelman, Outfitter and U.S. Forest Service trail crews.

Years of doing camp cooking for frequent family camping and hunting trips polished the trail cooking skills of MARILYN SUSEE of Tacoma, Washington. In addition to being a great cook, Marilyn enjoys cooking almost as much as she enjoys spending time in the mountains. So in 1977 when Marilyn and husband Roy bought a packing business and named it Susee's Skyline Packers, Marilyn was a natural to fill the cook's boots!

JAMES WATTS of Raymond, Washington, became a professional trail cook four years ago when he started his Watts-A-Llama? Leisure Treks. Already a good home cook and family trail cook, Jim eagerly adapted his talents to the special challenges of being a llama trek chef. Jim's years of experience as a mountain climber and backpacker in the Olympic National Park, where he leads his llama treks, also helped prepare him for his current trail cooking duties.

Trail Cooks' Favorite Recipes

"This dish satisfies even the largest appetite and keeps everyone satisfied when they have a long day ahead in the saddle," says Debby Gallie-Miller.

SAUSAGE AND EGG CASSEROLE

1 pound ground or link sausage
8 slices bread, cubed
6 eggs
3/4 t dry mustard
1/2 t salt
2 1/2 cups milk
2 cups grated cheese
1 can cream of mushroom soup
1/2 soup can milk
1 can, mushrooms, drained

Brown one pound ground (or link) sausage.

Put slices of bread (without crust and cut into small cubes) into a 12-inch Dutch oven. (Or use bread scooped from loaf used in making the "Sit-On" Turkey Sandwich.)

Drain sausage and crumble meat over bread.

Whip eggs. Add dry mustard, salt, and 2 1/2 cups of milk and beat together. Pour over bread and sausage.

Sprinkle cheese over mixture. Mix together cream of mushroom soup, 1/2 can of milk, and mushrooms. Pour over mixture (or heat and add as sauce over mixture after it is baked). Bake at 350 degrees for 45 minutes. Let stand 10-15 minutes before serving.

"My Dutch Oven Breakfast is a good recipe for beginners because the oven temperatures aren't as critical as with 'real' baking," says Marianne LeSage.

DUTCH OVEN BREAKFAST

1 pound bacon
1 two-pound bag frozen hash brown potatoes
18 eggs
8 ounces grated Cheddar cheese

Cut bacon into 1-inch pieces. Brown in 12-inch Dutch oven over medium cooking fire.

Remove bacon from oven. Pour off excess bacon fat and use remaining fat to brown the hash browns. Add bacon pieces to hash browns.

Beat eggs and pour over bacon-potato mixture. Put lid on Dutch oven and add coals to lid, keeping bottom heat fairly low.

When eggs are cooked, sprinkle cheese on top. Remove oven from bottom heat, return lid with coals to oven and bake until cheese is melted.

Serves 8 - 10

This recipe can be successful with as few as 10 eggs. Sausage or cubed ham can be substituted for the bacon. Also, onions and/or green pepper may be added for a 'new' taste!

"This breakfast is very easy to increase when you find out you have unexpected guests or extra hearty appetites," says Marva Mountjoy. "All you have to do is stretch the gravy by adding more flour and milk."

BISCUITS AND GRAVY

To make the gravy, you will need the following:

3 pounds bulk sausage
3/4 cup flour
Johnny's Seasoning to taste
6 cups milk

Brown sausage in large skillet or Dutch oven.

Add flour and brown it with browned sausage. Season to taste.

Add milk and thicken to desired consistency (add more milk if it's too thick, or more flour if it's too thin).

Serve over biscuits.
Serves 12

To make baking powder biscuits, you will need the following:

1/3 cup shortening
1 3/4 cups flour
2 1/2 t baking powder
3/4 t salt
3/4 cup milk

Preheat Coleman Stove Top Oven. Cut shortening into dry ingredients.

(Read on...)

Slowly add milk and knead.

Roll out and cut biscuits. Bake until golden brown.

Serves 6

This is a good breakfast to serve on a day when camp is moved because the meal clean-up is so easy.

Bill Buchanan says this is a good recipe to get yourself started with sourdough. The results are light and crispy without beating egg whites as in regular waffles.

SOURDOUGH WAFFLES

1 cup sourdough starter
2 cups flour
1 cup milk
3 eggs
1/3 cup oil
1 t baking soda

The night before, mix starter, flour and milk together in a glass or plastic bowl. (Do not use metal containers with sourdough.)

In the morning, replace the starter. Then to the waffle mixture add eggs, oil and baking soda and mix until smooth. This will be closer in appearance to thin bread dough than standard waffle or pancake batter.

Bake waffles as usual on cast iron waffle iron.

Ann Fonken offers her Sourdough Starter recipe to those who would like to start cooking with sourdough and enjoying its distinctive flavor.

ANN'S SOURDOUGH STARTER

Mix 2 cups flour and 2 cups milk into a batter. Sprinkle in 1/4 t yeast. Mix together and store in a non-metal container with loose fitting cover.

Store the sourdough starter at room temperature if it is used several times a week.

If used less often, store it in the refrigerator. Each time you use some of the starter in a recipe, be certain to add 1 cup milk and 1 cup flour back into the starter pot.

ANN'S SOURDOUGH PANCAKES

The night before, mix the starter with the milk and flour.

- 2 cups sourdough starter
- 2 cups milk
- 2 cups flour

(Remember to put 1 cup flour and 1 cup milk back into the sourdough pot.)

- 3 T sugar
- 1 t salt
- 3 eggs
- 6 T cooking oil
- Flour

(Read on...)

In the morning, mix the sugar, salt, eggs and oil. Beat until eggs are frothy. Add this to the sourdough mixture. Add enough flour to obtain desired consistency. Fry on griddle as you would for regular pancakes.

Makes 12 servings

"If you're in an elk camp or anywhere with cold weather, have warm butter ready or you'll tear the pancakes when you try to spread it," says Andy Mills.

ANDY'S SOURDOUGH PANCAKES

Add two cups of sourdough starter to three cups of flour, mixing together with three cups of lukewarm water.

Let it set overnight in a warm place, fairly close to the stove, particularly in cold weather camping. But it can't get hot, just warm.

In the morning, replace the two cups of sourdough starter and then to what you have left add two eggs, three tablespoons of sugar, three tablespoons of oil (corn oil or whatever oil you have for cooking), a teaspoon of baking powder, a teaspoon of baking soda, a dash of salt and cook them on a hot griddle.

"With this breakfast it's easy to increase the number of servings by adding fried potatoes or by using leftover boiled or baked potatoes from the night before," says Marva Mountjoy.

PASAYTEN STEW

- 4 cups diced ham or 2 pounds bulk sausage
- 1 large onion, diced
- 1 green pepper, diced
- 1 can mushrooms, drained
- 1/2 cup shredded cheese
- 2 dozen eggs, cracked and whipped in a bowl
- Salt and pepper to taste

Brown ham or sausage with onion and green pepper.

When tender, add mushrooms, cheese and eggs.

Scramble the mixture together and add seasonings.

Serve with toasted English muffin.

Serves 12

To make toast in the mountains, place a large griddle on the stove (or over coals). Heat the griddle, lightly sprinkle salt on the griddle and lay the bread or muffins on top of the salt. The salt keeps your bread up off the direct heat and it will toast nicely.

"This sandwich carries well in saddle bags or on a pack horse. Our guests love these sandwiches! If you can't find round sourdough bread, a long loaf will work well, too," says Debby Gallie-Miller. "Save the bread you scoop out to make the 'Sausage and Egg Casserole' for breakfast."

"SIT-ON" TURKEY SANDWICH

1 large round sour dough French bread
1/2 lb thin sliced turkey
3 oz sliced pastrami
3 large tomatoes
1 small jar marinated artichokes
1/4 lb cheese, thinly sliced
1/2 cup mayonnaise
1 purple onion, thin sliced
1 can (2 1/2 oz) sliced olives, drained

Cut bread in half horizontally (remove top). Hollow out, leave 3/4" thick.

Combine artichoke liquid and mayonnaise. Spread 1/3 mixture on inside of bottom bread shell, 1/3 on inside of top bread shell and 1/3 on filling when sandwich is half-filled.

In bottom half, layer with tomatoes, meat, onion, cheese, artichokes and olives, until mounded high.

Put top back on. Wrap in plastic wrap. Refrigerate 2 to 8 hours.

Just before serving -- SIT ON IT!! This is necessary! Cut into wedges and serve.

Serves 6

"These two recipes have come from friends of mine," says Marva Mountjoy. "We always serve our guests a tall glass of lemonade or a hot cup of coffee after a day of trail riding and these snacks can be prepared in a few minutes. The ingredients travel well. The chili dip is good for later in the trip when the fresh vegetables for snacks are gone."

HOT CHILI DIP

1 large can beanless chili
1 large jar Cheese Whiz

Heat the chili on low heat. Add the Cheese Whiz and stir until the mixture is the consistency you want for dipping.

Serve with large corn chips while dip is still warm.

Serves 15

SHRIMP CHEESE DIP

1 large package cream cheese
1 jar cocktail sauce
1 can shrimp

Place the block of cream cheese on a plate. Pour the cocktail sauce over the cream cheese and sprinkle the can of drained shrimp over the top. Serve this dip with a basket of crackers.

Serves 12

"This wonderfully flavored appetizer gets its distinctive taste from the sausage," says Marva Mountjoy. "Basque sausage -- called chorizo -- is the one thing that adds the unique flavor to many of the things I make. It's made with pork, paprika and other seasonings."

CHORIZO CHEESE BALL

2 chorizos, chopped, fried and drained
1 large package cream cheese
1/4 cup Parmesan cheese, grated
1/4 cup chopped green olives
1 T olive juice or wine

Mix all ingredients together and form into a ball.

Serve with a variety of snack crackers.

-THE COOK TENT-

"This salad is a good change-of-pace dish, especially after all the fresh vegetables are gone," says Marva Mountjoy.

FRUIT SALAD

- 1 20-ounce can pineapple chunks, reserve juice
- 1 11-ounce can mandarin oranges, drained
- 1 16-ounce can fruit cocktail, drained
- 2 apples, diced
- 1 small jar maraschino cherries, drain and slice
- 1 pkg. instant vanilla pudding mix

Mix all fruit together.

Dressing: Mix 1 cup pineapple juice (add water to make 1 cup) with pudding mix to dissolve. Pour over fruit, mix well. Let stand to blend flavors.

Serves 6

If they are properly packed, frozen foods can stay in the cooler box for four to five days, even in mid-summer temperatures.

Wrap frozen meat in newspaper for packing. Small Coleman or Gott coolers that fit inside the packing boxes can be used to store frozen foods for longer trips.

"Deer and guests enjoy this salad," says Debby Gallie-Miller. "When we have left-over salad we leave it out for the deer to come into camp at night and finish. It's the only recipe we have that we know guests and deer both enjoy!"

CABBAGE SALAD

1 head shredded cabbage
3 green onions, chopped
4 ounces slivered almonds
1 package Top Ramen noodles, crumbled

Mix above ingredients together in bowl.

4 T sugar
1 t pepper
2 t soy sauce
1 t salt
1/2 cup oil
1/2 cup rice vinegar

Combine above ingredients to make the dressing. Pour over salad just before serving.

"This is a nice change-of-pace salad that uses ingredients that travel and keep well," says Chuck Morrison.

APPLE-RAISIN SALAD

3 to 4 large apples
3 to 4 stalks of celery
1 cup raisins
1 cup salad dressing (like Miracle Whip)
3 T sugar

Cut celery and apples into small pieces and put into bowl. Add raisins and mix with apples and celery.

To salad dressing, add sugar and mix well. Pour over apples, celery and raisins and mix together.

Cover and keep refrigerated.

Serves 6

"This isn't like the usual 'slaw'," says Ann Henry. "This is quick to put together, very tasty and very refreshing."

OLD-FASHIONED CABBAGE SALAD

1/2 head cabbage, chopped
1/2 green pepper, chopped
1/3 cup white vinegar
3 T vegetable oil
2 T sugar
1 t instant minced onion
1 t salt
1/2 t celery seed
1/2 t dry mustard
1/4 t pepper

Mix together cabbage and green pepper.

In another bowl, mix the dressing ingredients together. Pour over cabbage.

Refrigerate for 3 hours either in the cooler or the creek.

Drain before serving.

Serves 6

"This is a good salad to serve toward the end of the trip," says Ann Miller, "because the cabbage lasts longer and survives bouncing around on a mule much better than lettuce does."

PEAS AND PEANUT SLAW

1 pkg. (10 ounces) frozen peas
2 cups shredded cabbage
4 green onions, sliced
1/4 cup sour cream
1/4 cup mayonnaise
1/4 t salt
1/4 t curry powder
Dash of pepper
1 t prepared mustard
1 t wine vinegar
1/2 to 3/4 cup peanuts

Mix together peas, cabbage and onion in bowl.

In separate bowl, combine sour cream, mayonnaise, salt, curry powder, pepper, mustard and vinegar and blend well.

Pour over cabbage mixture and toss lightly. Sprinkle with peanuts.

This may sound like an odd combination, but people seem to enjoy it. And it's easy to stretch for big groups -- just keep chopping and dumping!

"In a 10-inch Dutch oven, these biscuits will get fairly tall but they'll all fit. Serve them with butter and assorted jams and jellies," says Andy Mills. "Some people say not to use both baking powder and baking soda but I can't ever remember which one not to use -- so I use both."

SOURDOUGH BISCUITS

2 cups white flour
1 cup whole wheat flour
1 dash of salt
1 t baking powder
1 t baking soda
2 cups sourdough starter
Milk or beer

Take two cups of white flour, add salt, baking powder, and baking soda.

Add sourdough starter. Depending on consistency of the starter, add additional liquid. You can use milk but I prefer to use beer. Mix it up to a soft dough, then pour it out onto something to knead it. (I carry a cutting board with me on trail trips.)

Sprinkle whole wheat flour on a cutting board -- or on aluminum foil you can use to cover up a log, stump or board, depending where you're at -- and knead the dough until it's well mixed. Cut into biscuits, whatever size you want, or bake it into one big biscuit and then cut it up.

Use a 10-inch Dutch oven. Bake for 20-25 minutes at 350 to 375 degrees.

"I don't recommend baking this bread on the trail," says Jim Watts, "but I think this is the best bread to bring along on the trail. I developed this recipe myself so that I would get a bread that has a hard enough crust that it can be packed virtually anywhere, even top loaded."

TRAIL FRENCH BREAD

2 pkgs. or 2 T dry yeast
2 1/2 cups water (110 to 120 degrees)
6 cups unbleached white flour
1 t salt dissolved in 1 t water
Cornmeal

Dissolve yeast in water.

Measure 4 cups flour. Mix with yeast and water to make a sponge. Whip for 10 minutes with heavy duty electric mixer.

Add salted water and knead with mixer using dough hook for 5 minutes.

Place dough on floured surface and cover. Let rise for 2 hours.

Punch down and let rise for another 2 hours.

Punch down and mold into two "French" style loaves. *

Lightly cover bottom of bread pans with corn meal. Place dough in pans and let rise for 2 more hours.

(Read on...)

Bake in preheated oven at 450 degrees for 30 minutes. Have a pan of water on the bottom of the oven during baking time.

When baked, loaves should sound hollow when thumped. Remove from pans immediately and let cool.

When cooled, these loaves can be wrapped in aluminum foil and stored in the freezer for a couple of weeks. Don't slice bread until it is to be used.

* I use a bread pan that is designed to hold and bake 2 French loaves.

"Being able to serve toast with the meals is a 'nice touch' that the guests seem to appreciate," says Marva Mountjoy.

MOUNTAIN TOAST

Heat griddle on the stove or over coals. When griddle is hot, lightly sprinkle salt on the griddle and lay the bread or English muffin on top of salt.

The salt will keep the bread up off the direct heat and allow it to toast nicely.

"My Grandma Monte's recipe for Sheepherder's Bread is one of my favorites. Our Basque traditions say there is a cross cut into the top of the dough before it is baked and that the first bite of the bread goes to the sheepdog," says Marva Mountjoy. "On the trail I bake this into small loaves or rolls instead of using my Dutch oven."

SHEEPHERDER'S BREAD

3 cups water (hot)
1/2 cup butter or margarine
1/2 cup sugar
2 1/2 t salt
2 packages yeast
9 1/2 cups flour

Grease lid and inside of Dutch oven (Kitchen style oven #8 - 10-inch)

In a bowl, combine hot water, butter, sugar and salt. Stir until butter melts, then let cool to 110 degrees. Stir in yeast, cover and set in a warm place (about 12 minutes).

Add 5 cups flour and beat with wooden spoon. Add another 3 1/2 cups flour and stir into a stiff dough.

Knead on a floured surface about 10 minutes or until smooth, adding flour as needed.

Place in greased bowl, cover and let rise until double.

(Read on...)

Punch down, knead to form a smooth ball. Place in Dutch oven, put lid on.

Let rise until dough just touches the lid.

Bake in 375 degree oven with lid on for 12 minutes. Remove lid and bake 30 to 35 minutes.

"This recipe was created on an overnight trail ride with guests that had large appetites and I knew I didn't have enough breakfast for them," says Debby Gallie-Miller. "The reason it has vague measurements is that I have never really measured the ingredients. We have also added wild huckleberries when they are in season."

DUTCH OVEN COFFEE CAKE

Mix with a wooden spoon in a foil-lined, 14-inch, hot Dutch oven the following:

- 3 or 4 cups pancake mix
- 2 or 3 eggs
- 1/2 cup powdered milk
- Water enough to make a batter

Make a brown sugar, cinnamon, and butter mixture to crumble over the top. Bake at 350 degrees until done.

"Fresh baked biscuits go well with so many different dishes," says Marva Mountjoy, "especially in the wonderful outdoors."

BAKING POWDER BISCUITS

1/3 cup shortening
1 3/4 cups flour
2 1/2 t baking powder
3/4 t salt
3/4 cup milk

Preheat Coleman Stove Top Oven.

Cut shortening into dry ingredients.

Slowly add milk and knead.

Roll out and cut biscuits.

Bake until golden brown.

Serves 6

Marva says that a Coleman Stove Top Oven works better over a propane stove where heat can be regulated than over a sheepherder's wood stove. She's baked her favorite pies, cakes, cookies, muffins, biscuits, breads and potatoes in the Coleman oven. This oven bakes more slowly than a conventional oven, though.

For cooking ease on trips, pre-measure your baking ingredients and store in zip lock bags.

Marva Mountjoy enjoys preparing this colorful dish which is a family recipe from her Basque heritage. "My grandparents are from Spain and growing up with them I didn't even think about what they cooked as Basque recipes, that's just how they cooked and how I cooked. Just everything I do, I guess, is part of the Basque way."

BASQUE CHICKEN

20 pieces chicken
5 green peppers
5 red peppers
4 onions
3 cloves, garlic
3 cans stewed tomatoes
1 can black olives
1 jar green olives

Brown chicken in hot oil. Set chicken aside.

In same large, deep griddle, saute sliced vegetables and garlic until tender.

Add tomatoes and chicken, simmer 30 minutes.

Add sliced olives to mixture and heat.

Serve with rice.

Makes 15 servings

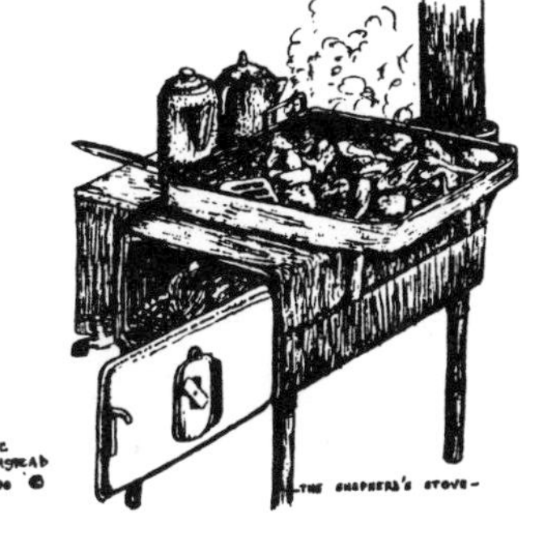

"This is a good dinner for the last night of a long trip when it's necessary to use the canned meat," says Sarah Parrington.

DUTCH OVEN CHICKEN ENCHILADAS

2 cans (12 1/2 ounces each) chicken meat
1 package corn tortillas
1 onion, chopped
1 green pepper, chopped
2 cans green chiles
1 can olives, chopped
1 pound Jack cheese, grated
1 can enchilada sauce
1 can cream of chicken soup
6 ounces sour cream

Mix together onion, green pepper, chicken meat, and 1 can chiles.

Fill tortillas with mixture and some cheese. Roll up and place in greased Dutch oven.

Mix together soup, sauce and sour cream. Pour over tortillas. Top with remainder of grated cheese, olives, and 1 can chiles.

Cover, bake in medium hot oven about 45 minutes. Good served with rice and salsa.

Serves 8

"This is a good casserole to make at home and bring along frozen," says Marva Mountjoy, "then just heat it in a double boiler."

MACARONI CASSEROLE

1/2 pound macaroni
1 pound ground beef
1 onion, diced
2 garlic cloves, diced
1 can mushroom soup
1 can tomato soup
1 can water
1/2 pound grated cheese
1 can pitted olives, drained and sliced

Boil macaroni in salted water until done. Drain but do not rinse.

Brown onion, garlic and meat.

In large pot mix soup and water together, add all other ingredients, salt and pepper to taste. Mix gently but thoroughly to combine ingredients.

Serves 8

A double-boiler tip from Marva Mountjoy: To improvise a double-boiler, add 1-inch of water to a large skillet. Set second pot (with food) in the skillet and cover with lid or tin foil. Do not let the skillet boil dry, add more water as needed. Using a double-boiler allows you to reheat food without the scorching that would occur over direct heat.

"I cook this one quite a bit on mountain trips and everywhere else," says Andy Mills. "And one of the great things about it is that it all cooks in one pot!"

METHOW CHICKEN & BEDSPRINGS

1/2 cube margarine
2 or 3 medium onions, chopped
1 pound fresh mushrooms, sliced
2 t thyme
2 T of granulated chicken
    bouillon, not cubed
2 cut-up fryers
1 small package spiral noodles
    (Bedsprings!)
2 cans condensed cream of mushroom soup
5 strips bacon
2 or 3 bay leaves
Red wine
Water
Salt and pepper to taste

Melt margarine in 12-inch, deep Dutch oven. Saute onions and mushrooms with thyme and chicken bouillon. Remove from oven, set aside.

In frying pan, brown chicken pieces. Place browned chicken in Dutch oven intermingled with uncooked noodles. On top of chicken and noodles, add sauteed onions and mushrooms. Cover with two cans mushroom soup, undiluted.

Lay strips of bacon on top of soup, place bay leaves on bacon. Pour in two soup cans of red wine and two soup cans

(Read on...)

of water. Cover Dutch oven and cook for one hour to one hour and twenty minutes or until chicken is done. Time will depend on heat.

Serves 8 - 10

—THE COOK TENT—

Sarah Parrington says that this can be easily adjusted for the size of your crowd and the size of your Dutch oven.

STUFFED CHILES

1 large can whole green chile peppers
Jack cheese
8 eggs
1/2 cup milk
1/2 cup flour
1 t baking powder

Fill peppers with strips of cheese. Arrange in bottom of greased Dutch oven.

Beat eggs and milk together. Add flour and baking powder.

Pour mixture over peppers.

Cover, bake with medium heat (350 degrees) about 45 minutes. Will be puffy when done.

Serves 6

"This recipe has had lots of names," says Ann Miller, "all very colorful but not suitable for print. So for now we'll just call it 'Tortilla-Beef Casserole'. This is a good dish to make at home, then freeze it for the pack trip or camping. Bringing it along frozen gives you a good dish that has a short preparation time. When you freeze it, don't put the chips on top."

TORTILLA-BEEF CASSEROLE

1 1/2 pounds ground beef
1 medium onion, chopped
1 can (1 pound) tomatoes
1 can (10 ounces) enchilada sauce
1 can sliced, ripe olives -- with liquid
1 t salt
Pepper, to taste
Garlic powder, to taste
1/4 cup salad oil
8 corn tortillas
1 cup small curd cottage cheese
1 egg
1/2 pound sliced Jack cheese
1 cup shredded Cheddar cheese
Crushed tortilla chips

Brown beef and onions in frying pan.

Blend in tomatoes, enchilada sauce, olives with liquid, garlic powder and pepper. Bring to boil, reduce heat and simmer, uncovered, for 20 minutes.

Heat salad oil in pan and saute tortillas, one at a time, a few seconds until softened. Drain on paper towels. Cut in half.

(Read on...)

Beat cottage cheese and egg together.

Spread one-third meat sauce in greased 3-quart casserole or Dutch oven. Top with one-half Jack cheese, one-half cottage cheese mixture, and one-half of the tortilla halves.

Repeat this layering process. Top with the final one-third meat sauce, the Cheddar cheese and tortilla chips, crushed.

Bake, uncovered, at 350 degrees for 20 minutes or until thoroughly heated and cheese is melted.

Makes 8 to 10 servings

"Rather than an exacting recipe, this 'First Night Chili Stew' is a wonderful combination of flavors that cooks into a rich, thick hearty meal," says Sarah Parrington. "It's perfect for the first night out because it's easy but tasty."

FIRST NIGHT CHILI STEW

? ground beef
? Polish sausage
? onions, chopped
? green pepper, chopped
? cans tomatoes, canned or stewed
? cans tomato sauce or paste
? green onions, chopped
? cans kidney and/or chili beans
? olives
? mushrooms
? cumin
? basil
? oregano

In large pot, brown ground beef and sliced Polish sausage with onions.

Add green pepper, canned or stewed tomatoes, tomato sauce or paste, green onions, canned kidney and/or chili beans, olives and mushrooms. Season with cumin, basil or oregano.

Cover, simmer 45 minutes or so until the rest of the meal is ready.

Vary amount of ingredients for number of people to be served.

"This is a popular dish with guests, especially when appetites have been sharpened by plenty of fresh air and activity," says Marilyn Susee.

CAMPFIRE BEANS

In large Dutch oven, brown together:

2 pounds ground beef
1 large onion, chopped

Into meat and onion mixture, add:

1 3-pound can B&M New England beans
2 15-ounce cans red kidney beans
2 15-ounce cans small onions, drained
2 15-ounce cans yellow lima beans
2 1-pound cans green baby lima beans
1/2 cup brown sugar
2 T vinegar
1 t chili powder
1 cup catsup
1/2 cup Karo syrup
1 T dry mustard

(Note -- Do not drain beans)

Mix all ingredients together. Bake at 275 to 300 degrees for 4 hours in open kettle.

This makes a "large" recipe.

"This is a variation of a smaller recipe given to me by my friend Akiko Kitada," says Jim Watts. "Although this can be made at camp, I prefer to cook it at home and freeze the sauce in double 1-gallon size zip lock plastic bags. Then I use the bags of frozen sauce as part of my refrigeration when planning and packing for my llama trips."

ORIENTAL CURRY

4 pounds beef round steak
Cooking oil
6 onions, diced
6 carrots, diced
6 cups raisins
4 t salt
10 t curry powder
3 quarts water
Flour

Condiments:
Chopped walnuts, pecans, sliced almonds, sunflower seeds and shredded coconut.

Trim bone and fat away from meat and cut meat into bite-sized pieces. In skillet, brown meat pieces in very hot oil, one layer at a time. Remove meat and saute onions in skillet.

Add browned meat and sauteed onions to large pot or Dutch oven. Add carrots, raisins, 3 quarts water, salt and curry powder.

Simmer 1 hour or until meat and carrots are tender.

(Read on...)

Thicken with mixture of flour and water.

Serve over freshly cooked rice.

Put out condiments for guests to add as they please.

Serves 15 hungry guests

If sauce is brought along frozen in the trail cooler, use on second or third day (before completely thawed). Thaw over very low heat, stirring constantly to prevent scorching.

"To cut down on cooking time on the trail, I like to bring this casserole made at home and frozen," says Marva Mountjoy.

HAMBURGER CASSEROLE

1 pound hamburger
1 onion, diced
1 can tomato soup
1/2 can water
1 can corn, drained
2 T chili powder
Salt and pepper to taste
1 can mushrooms, drained
2 cups noodles, cooked and drained

Brown hamburger and onion.

Add soup, water, corn, seasonings, mushrooms and noodles. Mix thoroughly.

Serves 8

"I first threw this stew together on the Fourth of July while camping at Three Forks Cabin in the Pasayten Wilderness. I used 'on-hand' ingredients and wound up with a great first-night-on-the-trail meal because it's fast to fix," says Marianne LeSage.

FOURTH OF JULY STEW

2 top round steaks or other cut
1 onion
1 green pepper
2 cans stewed or canned tomatoes
(or one of each)
1 large can mushrooms
1 can corn
1 package frozen peas
Cooking oil
Garlic salt and/or other
favorite seasonings
Instant rice, cooked

Cut meat into bite-sized cubes. Chop onion and green pepper. Brown meat cubes in a little cooking oil in a preheated Dutch oven. Add onion and green pepper and cook until onion is soft.

Cut canned tomatoes into bite-sized pieces if necessary. Add remaining ingredients.

Season to taste with garlic salt or seasonings of your choice.

Heat through and it's ready to eat, or simmer as long as you like until meat is tender, depending upon cut of meat used.

(Read on...)

Serve over rice. Serves 4 - 6, but easily expandable.

By substituting the new kinds of canned tomatoes with seasonings, for example Italian or Mexican, you can vary the taste. Use similar seasonings if any additional are necessary. The stew can also be "hotted up" with hot pepper sauce.

"For a real treat, try roasting beef in a Dutch oven. You will have the most wonderful au jus and beef that will melt in your mouth -- especially the baron of beef," says Debby Gallie-Miller.

ROAST BEEF OR BARON OF BEEF

Take a 14-inch Dutch oven (for a sirloin tip roast) or a 16-inch Dutch oven (for a baron of beef) and sprinkle pepper and garlic salt over the bottom.

Heat the oven directly over the campfire until the oven is very hot, then begin to sear the meat. Add more pepper and garlic salt as needed.

When the meat is seared, cover oven and bake meat using charcoal until it is done to your liking (rare to well done). It will take from 1 1/2 to 3 hours, depending on the size of your roast.

"This dish serves 8 to 10 people," says Andy Mills, "but on one trip a guy didn't like onions so it went a lot further than I thought it would!"

ONION CASSEROLE

4 - 6 large Walla Walla Sweet Onions *
2 cups grated cheese **
2 cups cracker crumbs
2 eggs
2 cups light cream (or half and half)
Salt and pepper to taste

Peel onions. Slice onions into a 10-inch Dutch oven. Add grated cheese and 1 1/2 cups cracker crumbs.

Mix all of this together and cover top with remaining cracker crumbs.

Mix eggs with cream, salt and pepper. Pour mixture over ingredients.

Cover and cook at 350 degrees for 20 to 25 minutes. Be sure not to overcook.

Serves 8 - 10

* The first time I made this I used regular yellow onions. They work just fine, but I prefer to use Walla Walla Sweet Onions.

** You can change the flavor by using different cheeses. Swiss cheese is mild, Romano cheese is a little more pungent, and Parmesan can be used, too. I prefer Romano.

"My family has always loved chili," says Dorothy Noblitt, "so over the years I have developed my own version. Coming back to camp and a bowl of steaming chili takes the chill out of any cool, camping evening."

DOROTHY'S CHILI

1 pound ground meat
1 medium onion, chopped
1 clove garlic, chopped
2 T chili powder
2 pinches hot red ground pepper
Salt to taste
1 t cumin
1 t oregano
1 t basil
1 8-ounce can tomato sauce
1 1/2 cans water (use tomato sauce can)
1 15-ounce can chili beans
1/2 cup Burgundy wine

In Dutch oven, saute together meat, onion and garlic until meat is done. Spoon off fat.

To meat mixture, add chili powder, hot red ground pepper, salt, cumin, oregano and basil. Stir well and add tomato sauce, water, chili beans and wine.

Simmer chili for 45 minutes to one hour. And, keep an eye on it, since you may need to add more water during the chili's cooking time.

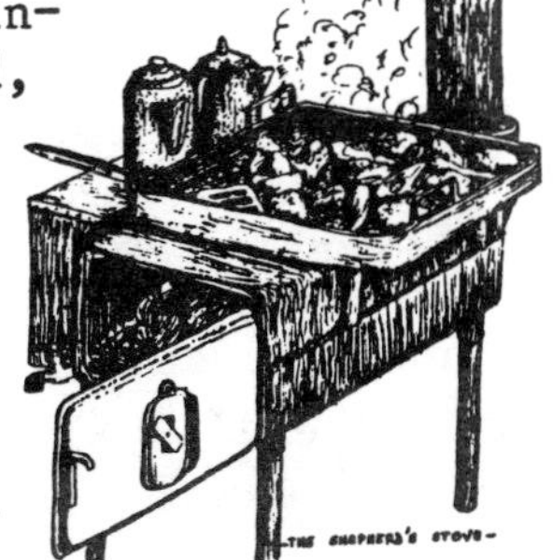

"Because of some packing weight restrictions with llamas," says Jim Watts, "I prefer to make this at home, freeze it in double 1-gallon size zip lock plastic bags and use it to help keep the other foods cool. If I were going to make it at camp though, I would trim the meat and cut it into cubes at home, then freeze it to bring along. The rest goes together easily. This is a recipe I developed myself through 'trial and error'."

BURGUNDY BEEF

4 pounds beef round steak
Bacon grease and olive oil to
make 4 T
5 cups Burgundy wine
2 cans tomato sauce
1 1/2 tomato sauce cans water
5 cloves garlic
6 shots Tabasco sauce
2 t or 2 cubes beef bouillon
1 t thyme
1 bay leaf
Salt to taste
1 pound fresh mushrooms, sliced
3 chopped onions
Roux of 1/2 cup flour and 1/2
cup margarine

Trim bone and fat away from meat and cut meat into 1-inch cubes. In skillet with very hot bacon grease and olive oil, brown meat one layer at a time.

Put browned meat and wine into large pot. Add tomato sauce, water, garlic, Tabasco sauce, bouillon, thyme, bay leaf, and salt.

(Read on...)

Cover and cook over medium heat for one hour or until meat is tender. In the meantime, saute together mushrooms and onions in separate pan.

When meat is tender, add mushrooms and onions, and cook for 20 minutes.

Then add roux, mixing and heating thoroughly. Sauce is now ready. Serve over fresh cooked rice or pasta. Serves 10 hungry appetites!

"I like this recipe," says Ann Fonken, "because none of the ingredients is perishable, so it's a great meal for the last day of a trip."

CHICKEN LINGUINE

1 medium onion, chopped
2 T olive oil
2 cans (10 ounces) boned chicken
1 can chopped ripe olives or mushrooms
1 large jar Ragu Garden Vegetable Spaghetti Sauce
1 pound linguine noodles
1 pound Cheddar cheese, grated

In a Dutch oven, brown chopped onion in olive oil. Add chicken, olives and spaghetti sauce.

Cook noodles and rinse in cool water and drain. Stir into spaghetti sauce and top with cheese.

Put lid on Dutch oven and put a few coals on top to toast and melt cheese.

Makes 6 servings

"All ages love this dish. It was developed at our Camp Wahoo! youth camp toward the end of the summer when we needed a change in our regular menus," says Debby Gallie-Miller. "It's a really simple dish, also."

TERIYAKI CHICKEN AND RICE

Into a hot, 14-inch Dutch oven place the following:

Chicken thighs or drumsticks
1 can crushed pineapple
1 or 2 red peppers, sliced
Fresh mushrooms, sliced

Sprinkle 1 cup or so of brown sugar over the top and pour in 1 bottle of soy sauce. (You may want to substitute your favorite teriyaki sauce for the soy sauce.)

Cover oven and bake until chicken is done.

Serve over rice.

To boil rice in a Dutch oven, place the rice and water in oven and set over campfire until water comes to a boil. Remove and set next to your campfire and let rice steam until fluffy. Makes perfect rice every time.

"This is a great dish to prepare in a Dutch oven," says Ann Henry. "The recipe is a favorite that I've used for years."

COLORADO BEANS

12 strips bacon
2 large cans kidney beans, rinsed
3 or 4 coarsely chopped onions
3 chopped green bell peppers
3 chopped medium tomatoes
 or 1 can stewed tomatoes
Small bottle ketchup
1 cup brown sugar
1 T prepared mustard

Place 6 strips bacon on bottom of casserole or 12-inch Dutch oven.

Put one-half rinsed beans on top of bacon.

Add vegetables, then rest of beans. Top with last 6 strips of bacon.

In bowl, mix ketchup, sugar and mustard. Pour over bean mixture.

Cover and bake at 325 degrees for 3 1/2 hours.

Makes 5 servings

—THE MAIN INGREDIENTS—
—DUTCH OVENS—

"I love cooking chicken. It's a favorite of mine. This recipe is really versatile because you can adapt it at least three other ways," says Chuck Morrison.

CHICKEN AND DUMPLINGS

1 chicken
3-4 onions
1/2 bag carrots, cut up
1 clove minced garlic
2 green bell peppers
4-5 small red potatoes
1 stalk, celery, cut up
1 cup frozen corn
1 cup frozen peas
4 chicken bouillon cubes
1 t sage
1 t Mrs. Dash seasonings
Salt and pepper to taste

Boil chicken, onions, carrots, garlic and peppers in water. When chicken is done, debone. Add other ingredients, bring to boil. Reduce heat and simmer for approximately 3-4 hours.

CHUCK'S DUMPLINGS

2 cups Krusteaz's pancake mix
1/2 cup margarine or butter (melted)
1/2 cup water
2 T sugar

Mix together. Let dumplings set for one to two hours to raise. Bring chicken mixture to boil (thin if necessary).

(Read on...)

Drop dumpling batter by heaping tablespoons onto mixture.

Cover with a lid. Add a few extra coals to lid. Cook 'til done.

Serves 6 to 8

To serve your chicken other delicious ways --

To chicken, vegetables and seasonings, add a package of chicken gravy mix and serve over mashed potatoes.

To chicken, vegetables and seasonings, add uncooked noodles and cook until tender. Add more water if necessary.

Simply serve chicken, vegetables and seasonings as soup, with crackers or biscuits.

Marianne LeSage says, "This recipe was first given to me by Vivian Hagaman. She and her husband Carl were charter members of W.O.G.A. and longtime outfitters in the Yakima area. She was the original secretary-treasurer for W.O.G.A. and held that post for the first six years of the organization's life, until I was elected in 1983 or so. This dessert is sweet and rich and always a hit in camp, especially after a long ride! The result never fails to impress people, considering the 'dump' method used. I think a lot of Dutch oven cooks use this recipe or a variation of it."

DUMP CAKE

1 box yellow cake mix
1 can fruit pie filling (cherry, blueberry or other)
1 8-ounce can crushed pineapple (do not drain)
1 cup butter, melted
1 cup pecans, chopped

Line 12-inch Dutch oven with heavy-duty foil. Dump pie filling and pineapple into Dutch oven. Dump dry cake mix on top. Dump melted butter on top of cake mix. Sprinkle pecans on top.

Put top on Dutch oven and add coals. Bake at moderate (350 degrees) temperature 30 to 40 minutes or until cake is browned and springy.

Makes 8 - 10 servings

"When our wranglers bake this one on trail trips all the women guests think the guys are wonderful cooks!!!," says Debby Gallie-Miller.

WRANGLERS' DUMP CAKE

Into a 12-inch hot Dutch oven, dump ingredients in this order:

1 can cherry pie filling
1 can crushed pineapple
1 package yellow cake mix (dry)
1 cup butter or margarine
(place slices over top)
1 cup coconut
1 package slivered almonds

Put lid on Dutch oven.

Bake at 350 degrees until cherry pie filling bubbles through and the top is a golden brown.

Variations --

Blueberry pie filling
and lemon cake mix

Apple pie filling
with spice cake mix

"This recipe came to me," says Marianne LeSage, "from my dear friend and riding buddy Elsie Crossland, who used it to successfully convince me that rhubarb is good to eat! It's quick, tasty and adaptable. What more could you ask of a trail recipe?"

ELSIE'S FRUIT COBBLER

For 10-inch Dutch oven, serves 6 to 8

1 cube (1/2 cup) margarine
Fruit filling
- 4 cups fruit
- 1 cup water or liquid
- 1 cup sugar*

Batter
- 1 cup flour
- 1 cup sugar
- 3/4 cup milk
- 2 t baking powder

For 12-inch Dutch oven, serves 8 to 10

1 1/2 cubes (3/4 cup) margarine
Fruit filling
- 6 cups fruit
- 1 1/2 cups water or liquid
- 1 1/2 cups sugar*

Batter
- 1 1/2 cups flour
- 1 1/2 cups sugar
- 1 cup plus 2 T milk
- 3 t baking powder

Prepare fruit. If using apples, peel and chop coarsely, then add a little cinnamon; if using rhubarb, then chop

(Read on...)

coarsely; if using fresh peaches, peel and slice; if using canned fruit, drain and reserve liquid.

In a saucepan, bring fruit to a boil with sugar and water (or liquid if using canned fruit).

Meanwhile, melt margarine in bottom of Dutch oven.

Prepare batter by mixing together remaining sugar, flour, baking powder and milk.

Pour batter into melted margarine in Dutch oven, then pour hot fruit mixture on top of batter. Put top on Dutch oven and add coals. Bake at moderate (350 degrees) temperature for 25-35 minutes.

* Sugar may be adjusted according to sweetness of fruit. This amount of sugar is enough for rhubarb or tart apples.

Fruits and vegetables pack well in plastic snap lock containers. Place a damp towel over the container to help keep them cool during hot weather trips.

For your camping convenience, use powdered milk whenever milk is called for in a recipe.

Be sure to pack out your empty cans and other camp refuse.

"These taste just like fresh doughnuts," says Marilyn Susee. "I found the recipe in the 1971 edition of the 'Professional Guides Manual'."

WILDERNESS DOUGHNUTS

Bisquick baking mix
Powdered milk
Crisco

Mix Bisquick and milk made from powdered milk. Batter should be thick.

Drop a thick spoonful at a time into hot, deep shortening. When golden brown, remove from shortening and drain on absorbent paper.

While still warm, roll doughnuts in sugar.

"This is a different kind of chocolate cake. I modified a Pillsbury Bake-Off recipe to get this version," says Sarah Parrington.

CHOCOLATE TRAIL CAKE

In the bottom of a 12-inch Dutch oven, melt and mix together the following:

1/2 cup butter or margarine
1/4 cup cream
1 cup brown sugar
3/4 cup chopped nuts
3/4 cup coconut

Prepare a box of Devil's Food cake mix [according to high altitude directions when you're in the mountains.] Pour batter over hot mixture in warm Dutch oven.

Cover and bake with medium high heat (350 - 400 degrees) for about 45 minutes. Use clean-knife test to check for doneness.

While still warm, carefully turn upside down - the nuts and coconut mixture becomes the frosting.

Serves 10 - 12

"This is a recipe inspired by one I found in 'Joy of Cooking' while looking for unusual sourdough recipes," says Bill Buchanan. "The sourdough gives this cake a distinctive flavor and it's not too sweet."

SOURDOUGH CHOCOLATE CAKE

6 T butter
1 cup sugar
2 eggs
1 cup sourdough starter
3/4 cup milk
3 ounces semi-sweet chocolate, melted
1 t vanilla
1 3/4 cups sifted flour
1 t baking soda
1/2 t salt

Mix ingredients together as given.

Line large Dutch oven with aluminum foil.

Pour cake batter into Dutch oven, cover and bake at 350 degrees until done, about 30 - 40 minutes.

(If you bake this cake at home, use a 350 degree oven -- 40 minutes for a 9 x 13-inch pan, 25 minutes for two 8-inch pans.)

An excellent topping for this cake can be made by mixing together a package of 'Lite' cream cheese and 1 small can chocolate syrup.

Marianne LeSage offers this Dutch oven dessert recipe for beginners. "The oven temperatures aren't as critical as with 'real' baking."

CROUTON COBBLER

1/3 cup margarine
2 cups plain croutons
1/2 t almond extract
1 can cherry, blueberry or other fruit pie filling
Cinnamon-sugar

Melt margarine in a pre-heated Dutch oven. Add plain croutons and stir into melted margarine to coat, adding more margarine if necessary. Remove 1 cup coated croutons.

Add almond extract to cherry, blueberry or other fruit pie filling and stir.

Pour filling over the croutons in the Dutch oven. Top with reserved croutons, pressing them into the filling. Sprinkle with cinnamon-sugar.

Cover and bake until hot and bubbly, about 15-25 minutes.

"I just mix my cake batter for this one right in my foil-lined Dutch oven, using a wooden spoon," says Debby Gallie-Miller. "Doing that saves washing an extra bowl."

CHOCOLATE RASPBERRY CAKE

Following the package directions, mix and bake a chocolate cake mix in a 12-inch Dutch oven lined with aluminum foil.

When baked, remove cake by lifting out the foil.

On top of warm cake, spread a can of raspberry pie filling.

Cut and serve cake with a dab of whipped cream on top.

To make whipping cream on the trail, use a package of Dream Whip, adding one half the amount of water called for. Whip with a fork.

"This is a family recipe that just seems to taste even better when cooked and served outdoors," says Sarah Parrington.

APPLE CRISP

Fill buttered Dutch oven with fresh peeled and sliced pie apples. Fill about 1/2 full.

(Read on...)

3/4 cup butter or margarine
3/4 cup brown sugar
1 1/4 cups flour
1/2 cup oats
1 t cinnamon

Combine above ingredients with fork until crumbly. Spread over apples in Dutch oven.

Cover and bake medium hot (350 - 400 degrees) for about 45 minutes until apples are soft and cooked through.

Serves 10 - 12 (Depending, of course, on the size of the Dutch oven used.)

"I use this recipe when I don't have a Coleman oven with me or when I need a quick dessert," says Marva Mountjoy. "This recipe uses ordinary staple ingredients, which is a real advantage."

NO-BAKE OATMEAL COOKIES

2 cups sugar
1/2 cup butter or margarine
1/2 cup cocoa
1/2 cup milk
1 t vanilla
3 cups oats (quick or old-fashioned)

Combine sugar, butter or margarine, cocoa and milk. Stirring constantly, bring to boil and boil for 3 to 4 minutes. Remove from heat, add vanilla.

Stir in oats. Drop on tinfoil.
Serves 18

"This is one of my kids' favorites. They always request it when we go camping. I guess they haven't figured out that I could bake it in the oven at home, too! But then, maybe they did figure that out but think it tastes better cooked and eaten outdoors!", says Marianne LeSage.

APPLESAUCE UPSIDE-DOWN GINGERBREAD

Line a 12-inch Dutch oven with heavy aluminum foil. Then, pour in about one quart of cinnamon-flavored applesauce, preferably made with Washington State Golden Delicious apples.

Position Dutch oven over moderate heat until applesauce bubbles.

Prepare a gingerbread mix. Pour gingerbread batter over bubbling applesauce. Put lid on and add coals enough to make moderate to high heat. Bake until gingerbread is done; usually 15 - 30 minutes, depending on the quality of the coals and the ambient temperature.

Serve hot with whipped cream. Smells and tastes delicious without being too sweet.

—THE MAIN INGREDIENTS—
—DUTCH OVENS—

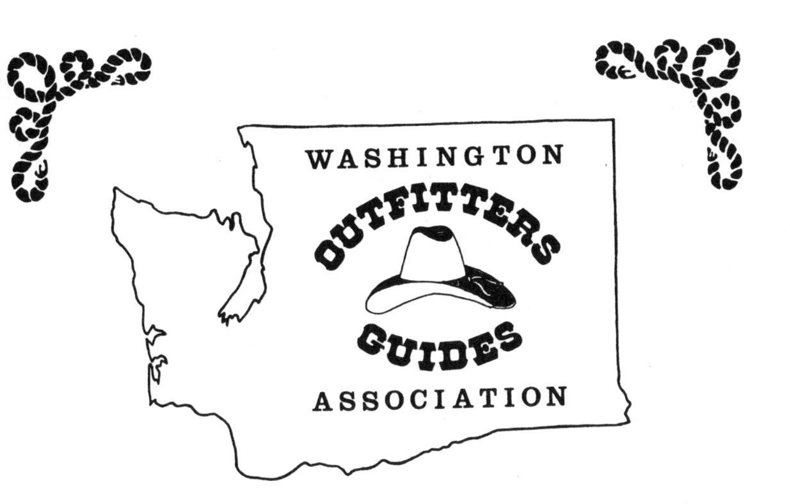

The Washington Outfitters & Guides Association was formed in 1978 to further the interests of all outfitters in Washington state.

In 1982 its brochure won the Governor's Award as the best travel brochure in its class. Through the brochure, association promotions such as the spring Outfitters Rendezvous each May and cooperation with news media, the group has increased the public's awareness of members' contributions to recreation opportunities in the Pacific Northwest.

The Association is also active in promoting the preservation, enhancement and shared use of the Northwest, particularly its designated wilderness areas.

W.O.G.A. maintains liaison with the U.S. Forest Service, Washington State Department of Wildlife and the State Legislature to lend its views and experience to solving today's many environmental and multiple-use issues.

The Association is a member of the National Forest Recreation Association.

Each member of W.O.G.A. adheres to a Code of Ethics that includes maintaining high standards of professional conduct, safe equipment and procedures, clean wholesome food and trained, experienced guides and trail crews. Outfitters are also subject to a variety of Federal and State regulations and laws established to govern their profession.

The W.O.G.A. outfitters have a variety of specialties -- from horsepacking trips into wilderness and U.S. Forest Service areas for camping and sight-seeing to hunting pack trips, day rides, half-day rides, rides by the hour, overnights, beach rides, llama treks and river rafting excursions.

In January 1991 the membership of W.O.G.A. was expanded to include all outfitters and guides in Washington state, including river rafting, sea kayaking, ski touring and mountain climbing guides and outfitters.

Brochures about W.O.G.A. and its members can be obtained by writing to Washington Outfitters & Guides Association, 22845 NE 8th, Suite 331, Redmond, WA 98053.

Washington Outfitters & Guides Association Members

BLUE MOUNTAIN OUTFITTING, INC.
Mark Huett, Route 2, Box 54A, Asotin, WA 99402

BRIAN VARRELMAN, OUTFITTER
P.O. Box 284, Pateros, WA 98846

CASCADE CORRALS - STEHEKIN VALLEY RANCH
Cragg Courtney, Box 67, Stehekin, WA 98852

CASCADE WILDERNESS OUTFITTERS
Steve Darwood, P.O. Box 103, Carlton, WA 98814

DOUBLE D WILDERNESS ADVENTURE, INC.
David Porter, 1251 Carroll Road, Kelso, WA 98626

DOWNSTREAM RIVER RUNNERS
Casey Garland, 12112 NE 195th, Bothell, WA 98011

EAGLE CREEK RANCH
Orvil and Sherry Huff, P.O. Box 719,
Leavenworth, WA 98826

EARLY WINTERS OUTFITTING
Aaron Lee Burkhart, P.O. Box 232,
Mazama, WA 98833

GRIZZLY MORGAN PACK TRIPS
Gene "Grizzly" Morgan
2901 S. Skagit Highway, Sedro Woolley, WA 98284

HAPPY TRAILS
Jack C. Price, P.O. Box 32, Easton, WA 98925

HIGH COUNTRY OUTFITTERS/CAMP WAHOO!, INC.
Swede and Debby Miller, 22845 NE 8th, Suite 331
Redmond, WA 98053

ICICLE OUTFITTERS & GUIDES, INC.
Bruce and Sandy Wick, P.O. Box 322,
Leavenworth, WA 98826

JORGENSON ENTERPRISES
Gerhard Jorgenson, PO Box 129, Duvall, WA 98019

KAISER'S MOUNTAIN ENTERPRISES
Leonard R. Kaiser, 18435 Highway 2,
Leavenworth, WA 98826

KIT'S LLAMAS
Kit Niemann, P.O. Box 116, Olalla, WA 98359

NORTH CASCADE OUTFITTERS
John Doran, P.O. Box 395, Twisp, WA 98856

NORTH CASCADE SAFARI
Claude Miller, P.O. Box 250, Winthrop, WA 98862

OLYMPIC PENINSULA OUTFITTERS AND GUIDE SERVICE
Jack E. Hutchins, 3595 SE Scofield Road,
Port Orchard, WA 98366

ORION EXPEDITIONS, INC.
James L. Moore, 1516 - 11th Avenue,
Seattle, WA 98122

PACIFIC CREST OUTWARD BOUND SCHOOL
Rita Kenny, 0110 SW Bancroft Street
Portland, OR 97201

SEAHORSE RANCH
Bruce Stewart, 5210 - 14th NW, Seattle, WA 98107

SUSEE'S SKYLINE PACKERS, INC.
Albert "Roy" Susee, 1807 E. 72nd Street
Tacoma, WA 98404

THREE QUEENS OUTFITTER/GUIDE SERVICE
D. L. "Cougar" & Janice C. Osmonovich
HC 61 Box 3040, Cle Elum, WA 98922

TIGER MOUNTAIN OUTFITTERS
Gary and Linda Schuler, 24508 SE 133rd
Issaquah, WA 98027

WILDWATER RIVER TOURS
Rod Amundson, P.O. Box 3623,
Federal Way, WA 98063

Pacific Northwest Guide and Outfitter Associations

IDAHO OUTFITTERS ASSOCIATION
P.O. Box 95, Boise, ID 83701

MONTANA GUIDES & OUTFITTERS ASSOCIATION
P.O. Box 1339, Townsend, MT 59644

OREGON GUIDES & PACKERS
P.O. Box 3797, Portland, OR 97208

WASHINGTON OUTFITTERS & GUIDES ASSOCIATION
22845 NE 8th, Suite 331, Redmond, WA 98053

About The Authors

John and Roberta Wolcott, owners of their writing and publishing business Features Northwest in Marysville, Washington, are full-time freelance writers and photographers who provide articles to newspapers and magazines on a variety of topics.

John has 28 years professional writing experience in the areas of aerospace, business, real estate, timber, energy, travel and public relations.

Roberta has 28 years experience in reporting, writing, editing, photography, and brochure and slide show production.

John and Roberta have published three previous books on writing topics and publicity for non-profit organizations.

Residents of Washington for three decades, they now spend much of their time writing about people and places across the state.

Their published articles on guides, outfitters and trail cooks have appeared in Northwest Living!, The Olympian, Puget Sound Business Journal, Cascade Horseman, Western Horseman and American Forests.

For additional copies of
TRAIL COOK BOOK, mail your payment to:
Features Northwest, P.O. Box 213
Marysville, Washington 98270

Name ______________________________
Address ____________________________
City ________________ State ____ ZIP ____

____ Copies of TRAIL COOK BOOK
@ $7.95 each........................$_____
Plus 7.6% Washington Sales Tax
(Residents only)....................$_____
Packaging & Shipping Fee................$ 1.50
Mailing Fee Each Additional Book/$1.00...$_____

Order Total: $_____

[Please allow 4 weeks for delivery.]

For additional copies of
TRAIL COOK BOOK, mail your payment to:
Features Northwest, P.O. Box 213
Marysville, Washington 98270

Name ______________________________
Address ____________________________
City ________________ State ____ ZIP ____

____ Copies of TRAIL COOK BOOK
@ $7.95 each........................$_____
Plus 7.6% Washington Sales Tax
(Residents only)....................$_____
Packaging & Shipping Fee................$ 1.50
Mailing Fee Each Additional Book/$1.00...$_____

Order Total: $_____

[Please allow 4 weeks for delivery.]